Tarantulas
Up Close

Carmen Bredeson

E| Enslow Elementary

CONTENTS

WORDS TO KNOW

fangs (FANGZ)—Sharp, pointed teeth.

palps (PALPS)—Small arms near a tarantula's mouth.

prey (PRAY)—Animal that is food for another animal.

spiderling (SPY dur ling)—Baby spider.

venom (VEH num)—Liquid from an animal that causes sickness or death.

Parts of a Tarantula (tuh RAN chuh luh)

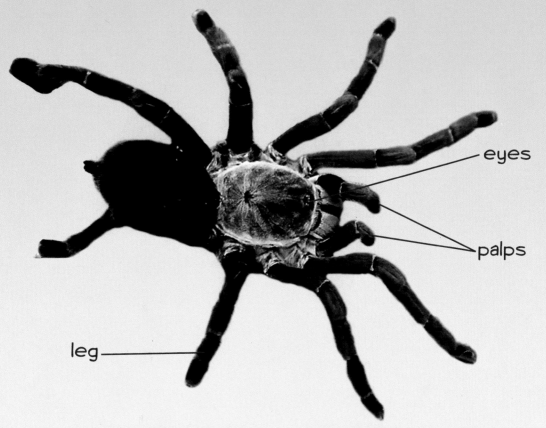

eyes

palps

leg

BIG TARANTULA

Tarantulas are the biggest spiders in the world. They live in warm places. Some tarantulas live under logs or in trees. Many make their homes in holes in the ground.

TARANTULA CLAWS

UP CLOSE

A tarantula has eight long, hairy legs. Each leg has two tiny claws on the end. There are many little hairs around the claws. The hairs help the spider hold on when climbing trees or walls.

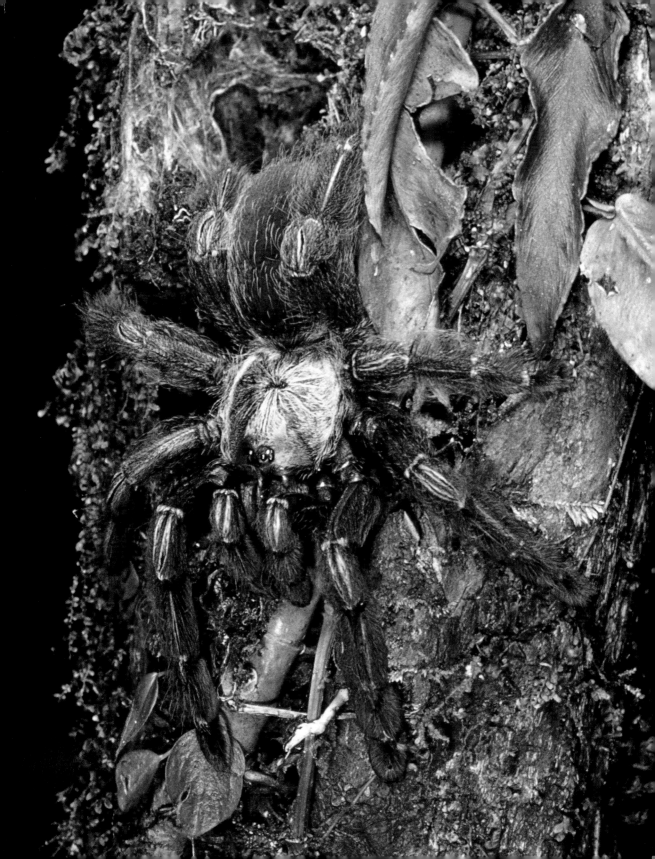

TARANTULA PALPS

Orange-knee tarantula

palp

There are two **palps** near a tarantula's mouth. The palps are like little arms. Palps hold food while the spider eats. Most palps have some sharp parts on them. The sharp parts are used to cut food.

Mexican redknee tarantula ▶

8

TARANTULA EYES

Tarantulas have eight eyes. Two are big, and six are small. Tarantulas may have a lot of eyes, but they do not see very well. They can see only light and dark or tell if something is moving.

Costa Rican tiger rump tarantula ▶

TARANTULA HAIR

Tarantula hair with sharp points (as seen under a microscope)

A tarantula is covered with hair. Special hairs on the spider's belly and back have sharp points. The tarantula can kick off these special hairs. The hairs fly through the air and sting the spider's enemy.

Young Antilles pinktoe tarantula ▶

TARANTULA PREY

The Goliath bird-eating tarantula is the biggest spider in the world. It can be twelve inches long.

UP CLOSE

Tarantulas eat **prey** like mice, birds, frogs, and insects. But tarantulas do not spin webs to catch food. Instead they hide in their homes. They sit very, very still and wait for prey to crawl by.

TARANTULA FANGS

UP CLOSE

When prey is near, the tarantula moves fast! Two sharp **fangs** stab the prey. **Venom** shoots into the prey to kill it. The venom turns the prey's insides to mush. Then the spider sucks up its meal. *Slurp. Slurp.*

This red leg tarantula is stabbing a cricket.

TARANTULA SKIN

old skin

Tarantulas have hard skin. They do not have bones. As a tarantula grows, its skin gets too small. The old skin splits down the middle of its body. Then the tarantula pushes the old skin off. The new skin gets hard.

Old skin of Ecuadorian
brown velvet tarantula

Tarantula with new skin

TARANTULA SPIDERLINGS

Tarantulas hatch from eggs. The **spiderlings** look like tiny eggs that have legs. The little spiderlings get bigger and bigger. They must grow new skin many times.

LIFE CYCLE

Tarantulas lay eggs in a silk ball.

Tiny spiderlings hatch a few weeks later.

Adult tarantulas can live as long as thirty years.

LEARN MORE

BOOKS

Eckart, Edana. *Tarantula*. New York: Children's Press, 2005.

Murray, Peter. *Tarantulas*. Chanhassen, Minn.: Child's World, 2003.

Parker, Steve. *100 Things You Should Know About Insects & Spiders*. Broomall, Penn.: Mason Crest, 2003.

WEB SITES

National Geographic
  <www.nationalgeographic.com/tarantulas>

San Diego Zoo
  <www.sandiegozoo.org/animalbytes/t-tarantula.html>

INDEX

Series Literacy Consultant:
Allan A. De Fina, Ph.D.
Past President of the New Jersey Reading Association
Chairperson, Department of Literacy Education
New Jersey City University
Jersey City, New Jersey

Science Consultant:
Thomas Bratkowski, Ph.D.
Professor of Biology
Maryville University
St. Louis, Mo.

Note to Parents and Teachers: The **Zoom In on Animals!** series supports the National Science Education Standards for K–4 science. The Words to Know section introduces subject-specific vocabulary words, including pronunciation and definitions. Early readers may need help with these new words.

Enslow Elementary, an imprint of Enslow Publishers, Inc.

Enslow Elementary® is a registered trademark of Enslow Publishers, Inc.

Copyright © 2008 by Carmen Bredeson

All rights reserved.

No part of this book may be reproduced by any means without the written permission of the publisher.

Library of Congress Cataloging-in-Publication Data

Bredeson, Carmen.
  Tarantulas up close / Carmen Bredeson.
    p. cm. — (Zoom in on animals!)
  Summary: "A close-up look at tarantulas for new readers"—Provided by publisher.
  Includes index.
  ISBN-13: 978-0-7660-3076-3
  ISBN-10: 0-7660-3076-8
  1. Tarantulas—Juvenile literature. I. Title.
  QL458.42.T5B74 2008
  595.4'4—dc22   2007025609

Printed in the United States of America

10 9 8 7 6 5 4 3 2 1

To Our Readers: We have done our best to make sure all Internet Addresses in this book were active and appropriate when we went to press. However, the author and the publisher have no control over and assume no liability for the material available on those Internet sites or on other Web sites they may link to. Any comments or suggestions can be sent by e-mail to comments@enslow.com or to the address on the back cover.

♻ Enslow Publishers, Inc., is committed to printing our books on recycled paper. The paper in every book contains 10% to 30% post-consumer waste (PCW). The cover board on the outside of each book contains 100% PCW. Our goal is to do our part to help young people and the environment too!

Photo Credits: Andrew Syred/Photo Researchers, Inc., p. 12; Brian Kenney/OSF/Animals Animals, p. 13; Darlyne A. Murawski/National Geographic Image Sales, p. 7; Francesco Tomasinelli/Photo Researchers, Inc., pp. 4–5; Gregory G. Dimijian/Photo Researchers, Inc., pp. 1, 8; John Mitchell/Photo Researchers, Inc., p. 14; Kenneth M. Highfill/Photo Researchers, Inc., p. 21; Minden Pictures/Mark Moffett, pp. 6, 15, 18, 19, 22 (top left); Nature's Images/Photo Researchers, Inc., p. 22 (bottom); Photograph by Richard Gallon, courtesy of the British Tarantula Society, pp. 10, 20, 22 (top right); Rhys A. Brigida, p. 3; Shutterstock, pp. 9, 11; © Steve Hoffmann 2007, p. 17; www.roamingcattle.com/tarantula, p. 16.

Front Cover Photos: Manny "the awesome" Lorras (left); Photograph by Richard Gallon, courtesy of the British Tarantula Society (center right, bottom right); www.roamingcattle.com/tarantula (top right).

Back Cover Photo: Shutterstock

Enslow Elementary
an imprint of
Enslow Publishers, Inc.
40 Industrial Road
Box 398
Berkeley Heights, NJ 07922
USA
http://www.enslow.com